THE
CARPENTER'S CHILD

Christmas Eve
Worship Service

BETTY LYNN SCHWAB

CSS Publishing Company, Inc.
Lima, Ohio

THE CARPENTER'S CHILD

ISBN 0-7880-0570-7   PRINTED IN U.S.A.

Lovingly and proudly
dedicated
to my son

Andrew

who, like Leah,
chose freely
to confirm himself
as one of
God's Own People

Table Of Contents

Introduction

About This Service

The Carpenter's Child is a Christmas Eve family worship service. It is 45-60 minutes long depending upon the other parts (solos or choir anthems, for example) that your congregation may want to include in this worship time. The service is built around a short story about a young girl living in Bethlehem at the time of Jesus' birth. The story is divided into two parts and set within a liturgy that lifts up ideas and themes from the story and weaves them together in the call to worship, prayers, offertory dedication and final blessing.

This entire service can be done very effectively by one liturgist who is also a good reader. Alternatively, while the liturgist does the service, a "readers' theater" style presentation would also work well with two or three readers sharing the complete story among themselves, seated on high stools in front of the congregation. A third option is to involve a whole group of people. In addition to the liturgist, there would be the Children's Moment leader, the scripture reader(s) and other people including any or all of the following: a narrator (who carries most of the story), Leah, Leah's mother, Nathan (Leah's friend), Hannah (Leah's friend) and Uncle Reuben.

No additional props are required. A backdrop, however, would be an effective visual focus, showing an Israelite home, and/or the village of Bethlehem, and/or the countryside at night. Partial or complete costumes would complement the narrative nicely, if the story is read as a play with speaking or silent "actors" involved. Subdued lighting enhances the sense of night, mystery and wonder and helps excited younger ones become a little calmer!

The Service of the Table (communion or eucharist) is not included in the Order of Service.

The Children's Moment is a necessary part of this service. Details for that Moment are carefully given. Thoughtful preparation is essential so that the leader is confident and comfortable with the ideas shared then.

About The Service And Story Theme

At Christmas time, we are all sensitive. We are sensitive to the sounds of Christmas carols. We are sensitive to the sights of colored lights over streets, around windows and on trees. We are sensitive to the smells of fires burning and favorite foods baking. We are sensitive to the taste of candy canes. We are sensitive to the feel of prickly pine trees, wet mittens, wrapped gifts, and a Merry Christmas kiss suddenly on our cheek from someone we love. We are also sensitive to people with less, to memories — painful and joyful — of Christmases past, and to facts of our present lives which we cannot change.

Yet in this very season, we can also be very insensitive.

Insensitive? Me? Us? At Christmas time? To what? To whom?

This worship service moves us gently and lovingly toward some answers to those questions. *The Carpenter's Child* tells the story of Leah, whose father — it is feared — has leprosy, that ancient, dreaded skin disease that numbs our limbs, making them insensitive even to pain.

What would your reaction be if that new member of your congregation suddenly shared with you that he had leprosy? How would members of your church react? Leprosy Mission International has excellent fact sheets to share with you and your congregation.

Leprosy of the body may seem too exotic a theme for Christmas. But what about leprosy of the mind (our insensitivity to new ideas) or leprosy of the heart (our insensitivity to the deeper needs of people today) or leprosy of the spirit (our insensitivity to God as God is active in our world today)? These kinds of leprosy (unlike leprosy of the body) are very contagious — especially at Christmas time. And, these kinds of leprosy (unlike leprosy of the body) are not eradicated by therapeutic drugs. They are eradicated only when we let ourselves be touched deeply by Jesus and when we then reach out as Jesus did and touch all others and indeed all creation in turn.

About The Story

This story is written, first of all, with a strong desire to remain faithful to the biblical accounts of Jesus' birth. No words are put into Mary and Joseph's mouths nor is any attempt made to enter their private thoughts or minds. Instead the story seeks to "flesh out" the setting in which Jesus' birth took place.

The story is written, secondly, with an equally strong desire for historical accuracy. The little details about house and temple construction, food and vegetation, the details about the religious attitudes and treatment of leprosy, and all the socio-economic details reflect — as accurately as possible — current scholarly studies about daily life in Jesus' day. The story is a pleasant way to learn about the authentic Bethlehem 2,000 years ago.

The story is also written with careful references to the children whose stories are told in other Christmas Eve services I have written and published with CSS: *Do You Hear What I Hear?, Sounds And Light Of Bethlehem* and *The Magnificat: Mary's And Ours.* Each service stands on its own. Continuity and depth builds, however, for those attending Christmas Eve services regularly. Children enjoy rediscovering familiar characters from the previous year. And yes they do remember — a whole year later!

May God bless us all as we reach out to touch one another in so many ways this holy season.

Saskatoon 1994

Christmas Eve Family Service

Prelude

Greeting

Processional Carol: "Angels From The Realms Of Glory"
(verses 1, 2, 3)

Call To Worship:

One:	Can you feel it?
All:	Feel what?
One:	The excitement in our holy room tonight?
All:	Yes! It's Christmas Eve. Nerves tingle! We sense something happening!
One:	Tonight we celebrate the birth of Jesus Christ, the One whose life reveals God's deep and lasting love for all.
All:	Oh, come let us worship God!

Carol: "Angels From The Realms Of Glory"
(Verses 4 and 5)

Prayer Of Approach *(in unison)*:
Holy God, you came to Mary and Joseph, to the shepherds and to the little village of Bethlehem. Come to us now, we pray. May our excitement tonight help us to be especially sensitive to you. Come, God! Be born in us this night. Amen.

Choir Anthem

Lighting Of The Christ Candle:

One:	For four weeks candles have been burning in our Advent wreath.
Youth:	One candle for Hope and one for Peace, one candle for Joy and one for Love:

These are God's gifts given to us through Jesus Christ.

One: Tonight we light the final candle, the candle symbolizing the Light of God we see in Jesus Christ.

Youth: This candle is white, the color of purity, as Christ's devotion was to God. This candle is at the center of our wreath, as Jesus is meant to be at the center of our lives.
(Youth lights candle)

All: Amen! Amen!

Youth: May our wreath and worship tonight help us remember Christmas all year long.

All: May our memories of this Holy Night help keep us sensitive to God all year long.

Youth: Amen!

Scripture Reading: Luke 2:1, 3-7

Carol: "Away In A Manger" (Verses 1 and 2)

Scripture Reading: Luke 2:8-20

Carol: "Shepherds In The Fields Abiding" (Verses 1 and 2)

The Carpenter's Child: A Christmas Story — Part 1

Choir Anthem

Moment Up Front: "He Touched Them"

Carol: "Silent Night" (Verses 1 and 2)

The Carpenter's Child: A Christmas Story — Part 2

Carol: "Silent Night" (Verse 3)

Offering: Our gifts for God

Offertory

Offertory Dedication: A Christmas Offering Hymn
(Tune: "It Came Upon A Midnight Clear")

Our Christmas offering we present
To You, oh Newborn One!
Bless it, we pray, and all the love
We have for You, God's Son.
Our world is deeply needing gifts
That only You can bring.
Help us, your people, heal the world
That all your praise may sing. Amen.

A Christmas Prayer And Blessing:

One: God of True Excitement, through Jesus Christ, you show us — like Leah — the happy and full kind of life you yearn for everyone to live.

All: We thank you, God,

Females: for our homes — new and old,

Males: for our family and friends who do not shut us out,

One: for our church who turns no one away,

Females: for the rewards of our honest hard work,

Males: for modern medicine that heals,

One: for scientists working to conquer all disease,

All: and for all the special moments in our lives we do not fully understand yet we remember.

One: God of True Health, you touch us at Christmas so that we in turn can dare to touch all others. Help us especially to reach out to —

Males: those whom we misunderstand,

13

Females: those whom we stereotype,

Males: those who are unwanted,

Females: our enemies and those who say mean things about us,

All: all whom we think are unclean in our time and place.

One: God of True Life, you care deeply for each of us, for all people and for all the earth.

All: Keep us sensitive! Keep us sensitive to
the despair and hope of others,
the unrest and peace in our world,
the pain and joy around us,
the hatred and love among us all,
the darkness and light within each of us.
Amen.

One: May the loving gaze of the Infant Jesus Christ, the healing touch of His Wounded Hands and the life-giving sound of His Risen Voice follow you tonight and echo richly within you and draw you to Him again and again.

All: Amen! Amen!

Recessional Carol: "Joy To The World"

Postlude

Children's Moment

"He Touched Them"
("Moment Up Front" in the Order of Service)

Background
Leprosy is one of the oldest recorded and least understood of all diseases. Centuries of fear, loathing, rejection and superstition have made the word "leprosy" a stigma. The word is no longer used by organizations like the Leprosy Mission.

The *New Catholic Encyclopedia* VIII (1967, p. 667-8) explains leprosy as "the only sickness whose traditional complex of social, legal, religious and hagiographical aspects have made its history inseparable from that of the Bible and the Church. It is unique also in that the treatment, cure and rehabilitation ... are impeded today by widespread errors ... associated with the Bible and the Church." Hence, there is a real need for worship leaders to help coax some of these errors and associations out into daylight throughout the Church Year. Christmas Eve is especially a gift or opportunity for the Church to do this coaxing since so many people come to worship only on that night.

Props For The Children's Moment
Use any toys, Christmas cards, notepaper, or small articles made by leprosy patients (readily available through any self-help type stores or outlets of the Mennonite Central Committee or similar organizations).

A small bookmark with a small piece of silkscreen print (from a leprosy hospital notepaper) glued on each could be made for each child.

Discussion
1. Review the story with children
   - Who is upset? Why?
   - What village does she live in?

15

- How do her friends treat her? Why?
- What explanation does her mother give?
- Do you think our God of Love would punish a family this way today?

2. Leprosy facts today
   - millions of people have the disease, 4,000 in USA alone
   - begins as small light patches on skin, insensitive to pain
   - curable through drugs
   - caused by a germ
   - it can deform a body badly when untreated

3. Christian spirituality of leprosy
   - In Bible, people with leprosy went to Jesus. Unlike everyone else, Jesus looked at these people, talked with them, touched them (most important) and healed them.
   - We need to be like Jesus in our thinking about people with diseases we fear today: i.e., be compassionate, sensitive, helping them heal.
   - We ourselves probably do not have leprosy of the body (all parts of our body are healthy and sensitive to heat, cold, pain).
   - But what if we are insensitive in our minds to new truth (leprosy of the mind) or in our hearts to people in need (leprosy of the heart) or in our spirits to God alive in the world as it is today (leprosy of the spirit)?
   - The better we know Jesus, the more we experience Jesus touching and healing us in all our personal insensitivities.
   - Give out bookmarks to help us remember Jesus when we feel shut out by others or when we are insensitive to other people, truth or God.

The Carpenter's Child: A Christmas Story

Part 1

"Why Bethlehem?" Leah sighed. "A tiny village like ours! Everyone knows everyone else and everyone else's problems. Why did Daddy have to get sick here in Bethlehem?"

The leather thong on her sandal had come loose. Leah raised the edge of her long blue robe, tightened the thong and then adjusted the woolen cloak around her shoulders and head. Leah was on the roof of her home in Bethlehem. Built just five years ago, her house was one of the new houses in Bethlehem. Unlike the whitewashed cube her family used to live in, this new house had a fine inner courtyard and a series of small rooms — some even with a window — built around the courtyard.

Leah remembered how her family had built their new house. Leah's father was a carpenter and had always been a hard-working man. When King Herod began building the new Temple in Jerusalem, her father did much of the outer woodwork of the Temple structure and some of the work in the women's court. It had meant days and weeks in Jerusalem, away from the family. But now the work was finished and Leah's father lived all the time in Bethlehem with the family — until "it" happened.

Until "it" happened, the family was happy about their father's extra work. They decided they could afford to rebuild their little one-room home. First the old house was levelled and most of the garden dug up (all but the fig tree and the new rosebush). Then the foundation was dug with great care. Her father insisted their new house would be built on bedrock. "Lest the wind and rain carry away our home," he had said over and over as he dug with those helping him. Then the walls were raised. No wattle and daub like their old cube house,

17

but bricks! Clay bricks Leah herself helped to make. She remembered how they piled the muddy clay together and wet it. Then she and her family mixed in the straw with their bare feet until it was just right. Then the clay was shaped into bricks and baked in the sun and the village oven. When dried, the bricks were piled carefully to form the outer walls and then the inner rooms around the courtyard.

Leah drew her finger down a line of mortar. She had helped make the mortar, too: tempered clay mixed with seashells (Uncle Reuben brought them all the way from Joppa) and ground potshards. Then came the floors — not just beaten earth like in her old cube house. No! Instead pebbles and some baked tiles! Leah had worked with her daddy as he patiently laid the pebbles and tiles. Then the outside staircase and roof were built. They couldn't afford tiles for the roof. Instead wattling was laid with just enough slope to carry off the rain. Then the woven sticks were covered over with beaten earth. For four years since, Leah helped her daddy care for the roof, repairing it every year before the rainy season. But it was a roof all the same — just right, Daddy said — for protecting their new house.

Often she and her daddy went up to the roof in the cool of the evening after sunset. Together they would gaze out over their village of Bethlehem. Her daddy kept his larger tools there on the roof in the dry season although tonight only an old axe remained. The rest of his tools were all stored away in an alcove of the wall until he came back — if he ever did. Leah shivered. The laundry for the day was also on the roof, although long ago dried.

Her mother was cleaning up from the evening meal in the courtyard below. She must have forgotten the laundry. No doubt she'd send Leah up to fetch it later that night. Leah didn't mind. Nothing mattered anymore.

Leah remembered the hours in the evenings she spent with her father up on the roof. After he went to the evening service at the synagogue, he'd give his special little whistle call to let her know he was back and together they'd climb up onto the roof. Each shared with the other about the day. Sometimes they'd read from the *Book of Prayers* her father loved so much. Sometimes her father would play his wooden flute and sometimes they would just sit together. It was their time. She loved every minute of it. How she missed him!

Just when everything seemed to be going well! She had been so happy: all Daddy's extra work, their new house, then the birth of the twins — both boys — and three years ago another boy, happy little Benjamin! After having just one daughter all these years, three boys! Now her father's name could carry on! Everything was going so well.

Then Uncle Reuben came for a visit. One stupid visit! Why did he have to come? Reuben and Leah's daddy had gone for a long walk out to the Shepherds' Field. Coming back her daddy fell, cutting his knee on the sharp rocks of the path. That's when Uncle Reuben noticed it. While her father bent over, lifting his long tunic to wipe his knee, Reuben spotted the white patches on her father's ankles, feet and knees. Uncle Reuben said he must have gotten them while working at the Temple with all the foreigners King Herod hired.

Her father hadn't paid any attention to the patches before. Suddenly they were the focus of the whole village. Patches of dry, whitish skin on his knees, more on his ankles, feet and elbows. Her daddy said the patches felt normal, only a little scratchy sometimes, like pins and needles. Uncle Reuben insisted he had to go immediately to the rabbi. The Holy Law of God required it! Else all of the family and the village might get the patches, too. So her father went to the rabbi, and that very afternoon the rabbi declared her father unclean! Unclean! Unclean! He never came home again. The rabbi said he had to go away immediately. To the wilderness, probably, with the other lepers and wild animals! For seven days and then seven days more! That was two weeks and two days ago. Where is Daddy now?

Now everyone in Bethlehem knew her daddy was unclean. For 16 days and nights no one came to their new house. No one talked to her mother at the well. No one greeted her in the market. Everyone was afraid they might get the patches, too. Everyone was afraid.

And now came the census. The Romans wanted more taxes. Everyone had to go to the place of their birth to be counted in the census. But none of her relatives — not even Uncle Reuben — came back to her house. Oh. They're here in Bethlehem, Leah sighed, but staying with someone else. The village was so crowded. Roman soldiers, donkeys, camels and people were everywhere. But no one came to stay with her family. They're all afraid. Afraid of getting leprosy.

Well, who cares? She didn't have leprosy. Mommy didn't have leprosy. The boys didn't have leprosy. They had each other and their new house!

Leah ran her finger again along the mortar and at this moment heard her mother's voice calling her.

Leah scrambled to the edge of the roof and down the outside staircase. Her mother was angry.

"Leah! I've called you and called you. Why didn't you answer?"

"I'm sorry, Mommy. I was thinking about Daddy."

"That's enough, Leah! We don't speak of that. Auntie Deborah has cucumbers, onions and cumin for us. She told me to send you over once it's dark. Run now and get it for us, please."

"But Aunt Deborah lives over by the inn, on the other side of the village! Look at all the people and soldiers! It will take me so long!"

"I know, but Aunt Deborah is waiting. She'll have the basket hidden for you right behind their fig tree, so you needn't go in the house or talk with her ..."

"I know," Leah interrupted. "They're afraid they might get it from me ..."

"Now calm, my little one. God is punishing us. It is God's will. We have done something wrong. Daddy has offended God."

"Daddy did nothing wrong," again Leah interrupted. "Daddy is a faithful Jew, one of God's own Chosen People, a good man. He observes every Sabbath and every festival. He goes to prayers every day at the synagogue and hasn't missed one sacrifice at the Temple; he tithes every fig from our tree and every piece of work in his shop; he gives to every beggar; he is a good man to his workers and he set our slave free in the seventh year. Daddy did nothing wrong! Why did God punish him with leprosy? God is unjust.''

"Leah! Stop! You blaspheme the name of God. God does only what is right and just. We must accept it and endure. Now go! And go quickly. I will be waiting for you to return. I love you, Leah! So does your father. Wherever he is ...''

Her mother went back to the courtyard. Leah slipped away from the staircase into the crowded maze of crooked streets.

Part 2

Out in the crowded village streets, six Roman soldiers, their spears striking the ground as they marched past, nearly knocked Leah down as they went. Donkeys, people everywhere, the intricate maze of streets seemed even more confusing than ever. But up alleys, along passageways and down lanes Leah made her way, dodging the crowds and animals. "Maybe I should cover my face and call out, 'Unclean! Unclean!' Then they would let me pass. What if Daddy never comes back? How will we live? Will Mommy have to sell me to feed the boys? Who would buy me now? Maybe Mommy would have to be married by Uncle Reuben. That's God's Law, too! But! That must not happen! Why? Why did Daddy have to get sick in Bethlehem?''

Tears ran down Leah's cheeks as she continued to dodge soldiers, donkeys, camel caravans and crowds. At length she reached Auntie Deborah's house. Immediately she saw the basket sitting in the alcove half hidden by the fig tree. "Even Auntie Deborah won't look at me ... She must have seen me coming and ran out just to put the basket there and then ran back inside. Don't worry Auntie, I won't touch you or your house! Neither you nor your house will get leprosy from me!'' As she stooped to pick up the basket, tears slid down her cheeks.

"Oh, Daddy! Will I ever see you again? I don't care if you have leprosy! I still love you.''

By now, Leah, basket in hand, was walking slowly, weeping and talking to herself. As she passed the Bethlehem Inn, Mr. Zadock's Inn, she heard sounds of laughter, singing and dancing. "At least someone's happy.'' Leah thought to herself. "I suppose even the inn would empty if I walked into it.''

Just at that moment her friends, Samuel and Tamar, darted past her without seeing her. Close behind came Nathan and Hannah, two other friends. They ran out the lane by the Inn.

The three children nearly collided into each other. Hannah quickly grabbed Nathan's arm and jerked him back away from Leah.

"It's Leah! Her father is the leper — remember what Mom said about her! Get away from her!''

"But,'' Nathan said excitedly, "Leah, Leah must know, too! Leah!'' he said, jerking away from Hannah and turning to Leah. "There's a baby. A baby's been born in the shepherds' cave right over there. We're going to tell everyone. Go and see him! This is a very special baby! Even Amon and Jonathan and the other shepherds saw bright lights in the sky and came to see the baby. They said angels told them to come! Go, Leah! Go see the baby and look at the light all around him. We're telling everyone!''

Nathan and Hannah ran off into the darkness.

"A baby born in the shepherds' cave?'' Leah was puzzled. "Me go and see him? Angels talking to the shepherds? A light in the sky and all around the baby? Maybe I'll go have a peek.''

Leah turned into the lane that went past the inn and over to the shepherds' cave. Nathan was right. Several shepherds were there. Leah stood at the mouth of the cave. Suddenly she caught sight of Benjamin, the young son of Bethlehem's rabbi. He was right up by the baby, talking to the mother and father. Instinctively Leah slipped into the shadows along the walls of the cave, hoping to avoid Benjamin's gaze. As she lingered, trying to get a glimpse of the baby, Leah felt herself relax.

Still hidden by the shadows, taking little step by quiet step, she slipped up along the cave wall as far in as she could go without being seen. "Heh! Even Sapphira is here! Her, one of them! People of the Land. Worse than pigs, the Rabbi said. Well, even she's better off than me now!"

Leah watched Sapphira kneeling by the manger, gazing at the baby for what seemed like a long time. At length Sapphira slipped quietly out of the cave. Leah could now see the swaddled baby lying in the manger. A soft light seemed to fill the space where he lay. As Benjamin and the shepherds spoke with the parents, Leah fixed her eyes on the baby. The baby was awake and at moments seemed to look right at Leah. "At least that baby doesn't look away from me like everyone else!"

She gazed back at him for a while. Leah was peaceful and calm now for the first time in 16 long days. As she lingered and gazed at the baby, somewhere deep within her she began to grow confident. Everything would work out. Everything would be all right. For now, she just loved to be here by this baby! Resting in the shadows of the cave, she soaked up all the assurance and tranquility the baby's gaze seemed to stir in her. She stood there for a long time. Her anger and fear melted away. She didn't know how things would work out, only that they would. After all, she was also one of God's People and God loved her. God would take care of her.

As silently as she had come in, Leah slipped out of the cave, confident and at peace. Puzzling over the change within her, she turned her back on the noisy, crowded streets and headed home by the narrow pathway leading all around Bethlehem, the one her father tripped on 16 days ago. Under the starry sky, she looked out across the Shepherds' Field and the large flock of sheep. Maybe an angel did tell the shepherds. But who could that baby be? Benjamin said something about the Messiah? The Messiah? Born here? In our village? Oh, Benjamin was always being so religious.

Just then Leah's Uncle Reuben came running up the path. "Leah! Leah!" he called to her. "I've been looking everywhere for you! Come home! Good news! Your father doesn't have leprosy. The priest examined him after the 14 days were up. The white marks had not spread. The hairs remained black. The priest declared him clean and sent him to the Temple at Jerusalem to complete the purification sacrifices required by the Law of the Leper on the day of his cleansing. He is on his way now from Jerusalem and will be home soon. Come! Leah, it's all over!"

Much to her surprise, Leah said nothing. Joy, peace, hope, love flooded her. The baby. The light. The angels. Now Daddy home. This was **one** night she would **always** remember. She could hardly wait to see her daddy. He would be the first one she'd tell about the baby. Maybe he'd go back with her and they could see the baby together ... Maybe Daddy would even know who this baby really is ... And why Bethlehem ...